BEFORE THE ROOSTER CROWS

A WALK WITH PETER THROUGH FAILURE AND REGRET

by

Dr. CHUCK GLENN

BEFORE THE ROOSTER CROWS
A Walk With Peter Through Failure and Regret

Copyright © 2021 by Dr. Chuck Glenn
Published by Moments with Yahweh

ISBN: 978-1-7341362-1-0

All rights reserved. No part of this publication may be reproduced, distributed, or transmitted in any form or by any means, including photocopying, recording, or other electronic or mechanical methods without prior written permission.

Scripture quotations, except where otherwise indicated, are taken from the New American Standard Bible:1995 Update, Copyright © 1960, 1962, 1963, 1968, 1971, 1972, 1975, 1977, 1995,
by The Lockman Foundation. Used under the guidelines of Zondervan.
All rights reserved worldwide. www.zondervan.com

Dr. Chuck Glenn
mwy4chuck.com
contacts@mwy4chuck.com

Like us on Facebook @ Moments With Yahweh

Dedication

To Alfred (Jack) and Edith Glenn

Thank you for all your wisdom! You are with our LORD, but you live on in my heart.

Acknowledgments

No book is written by one individual, it takes a small army to bring a concept to publication. I hope I have included everyone involved in this project. If I have missed anyone, please forgive me. First and foremost is my Proverbs 31 wife, Zeny, who has stood beside me as I struggled to write from behind my carefully crafted walls, and who painstakingly worked behind the scenes to bring this book to life. Bell, our teenage daughter who put up with my need for silence. Your patience is amazing! Philana, who challenged me to take my creative writing skills and use them for the LORD. Daryl and Kelvin, my accountability partners who have been involved in talking through all phases of this book. Pastor Scott Wiles, without his influence this book would still be sitting in the computer. Chris, Charity, Shanda, and Trina for believing in me. Brooke, who has walked with me through every stage of this book. The Just Digging Deeper small group that willingly went through this study and provided much-needed input. A special thanks to Debbi who came up with an amazing title. Most importantly I want to thank my

LORD and Savior Jesus Christ, who died that I might live. You left this earth to sit at the right hand of the Father, making way for the Holy Spirit who has given me a tremendous spiritual gift and talents galore to go along with it.

Forward

We all have regret. We all have doubts and fears, usually caused because of the regret and shame we carry from our past. Our past regrets from years gone by or even those from yesterday can cripple us spiritually. It doesn't matter who you are. Our past sin can haunt us. I know this is true in my life, and as I continue to minister to God's people, I realize that I am not the only one who needs God's grace, mercy, and forgiveness in this area. What is truly comforting is to know that all of the great men and women of the Bible also needed God's grace, mercy, and forgiveness.

The Apostle Peter, the rock, was no exception. The Bible study you are about to embark on is a wonderful study of God's grace in the life of the apostle Peter. My good friend, Dr. Chuck Glenn, has put together a wonderful study of how God's grace, mercy, and forgiveness abound in Peter's life from the time he denies Jesus to the point Jesus restores him on a beach during a breakfast of fish and bread. This study is impactful not only because it chronicles this specific time in Pete's life, but because like me; like you; Dr. Glenn has also experienced God's grace and forgiveness. It is Dr. Glenn's willingness to be transparent and allow God's Word to transform his own life that makes this study so impactful.

Dr. Glenn's knowledge of the original languages of the Bible opens great insight into how you will understand God's Word in this study. Dr. Glenn's knowledge of God's Word and the care he takes in presenting it to the reader in a way that is personal and understandable is a great asset to this study as well.

I hope you take the time to prayerfully engage in this study with a group of your brothers and sisters in Christ. I know it will be transformative for you. Allow God's Word and the discussions that Dr. Glenn will lead you through, lead you to the reality of God's grace so that you will no longer be enslaved to regret, doubt, and fear. My prayer is that you will be encouraged to share this message of hope to all those God brings into your life.

Your Brother in Christ,
Pastor Scott E. Wiles
Calvary Community Church

TABLE OF CONTENTS

INTRODUCTION-- 9

LESSON ONE: TRUST-------------------------------------12

LESSON TWO: BOLDNESS-----------------------------21

LESSON THREE: SELF-CONFIDENCE----------------31

LESSON FOUR: HOPELESSNESS/SELF-

                    CONDEMNATION-------------------39

LESSON FIVE: RESTORATION-----------------------51

CONTACT INFORMATION-------------------------------64

INTRODUCTION

The sound of soul-wrenching anguish embarrassed those whose eyes glanced off the hunched over man. The crowd's reaction was mixed as some pretended to ignore the man, others glanced away, while the majority hurried away from the scene. No one knew what had happened, but they could see the results.

The man pressed balled fists against his eyes struggling with the black despair of shame, guilt, and regret that threatened to engulf him. He looked at the pool of tears on the ground and wrapped his arms around himself as uncontrollable tremors shook his body. Peter's thoughts swept back to those few minutes at the charcoal fire in the courtyard. "How could this happen? How could I give in so easily? Why did I run away so fast?" As the soul-crushing truth of his failure kept assaulting him, he knew within the very depth of his soul that he was a failure. Those that were near heard him mumble, "I have no future, no hope. I know that Jesus can never use me again after I deserted Him." The mere thought of his ruined relationship with Jesus of Nazareth engulfed Peter in hopeless despair and the uncontrollable sobbing shook his body once again.

Have you ever felt that your relationship with Jesus has been ruined? I know I have. I've been supremely confident, standing firm as a rock assuring Christ that I would never waiver; never damage His cause, only to find myself alone, sobbing and racked with guilt as I viewed the shattered pieces I made of my life. Maybe you regret lost opportunities, losing control of your tongue, or failing in some other area of your life. Now you believe your relationship with Jesus Christ has been ruined, damaged, or hampered by those recurring thoughts of failure. We may sit in a congregation, lead a small group, or in some other way serve the Lord, yet we feel despicable because of our past. Whether we have hidden skeletons, feelings of guilt and remorse, a weight of regret, or a past we feel makes us unworthy to serve Christ, all of us can learn from Peter's journey.

In this study I want us to step inside Peter's shoes. I want us to try and feel his struggle in trusting Jesus, understand his boldness, and deeply relate to his hopelessness and self-condemnation. I want us to consider how we would feel if we were Peter and came face to face with the One we cursed and denied. What could we expect Christ to do as He brings us face to face with our ultimate failure and what is the outcome?

LESSON 1

Trust

Introduction:

Brent, a member of his university's Reserve Officer Training Corps (R.O.T.C.), calmly watched as a very scared freshman prepared to die. At least that is what her saucer-shaped eyes told him as she was hooked up to the rope on the thirty-five-foot-high rappelling tower. Brent's relaxed gaze was warm and friendly as he looked into her hysterical eyes. His smile carried a warm assurance as he gently told the young cadet to loosen her rear hand and press an "L" against the side of the tower. Her ridged body robbed her of the ability to speak, but Brent had no trouble understanding the intense side-to-side shake of her head. He pressed an "L" against the side of the tower and took a few steps down.

Brent kept his eyes soft and voice calm. "Trust the person on the end of the rope, if you start to fall, she'll stop you."

The frightened cadet quickly glanced at the tiny object below, then looked back at him with eyes made wide by unbelief. Her look let Brent know that deep within her soul she knew trusting the speck below made absolutely no sense.

What if I told you that Peter faced the same situation regarding trust? He was asked to do something that made absolutely no sense.

Before we begin, let's read these passages to gain an understanding of this event.

Lesson Text: Luke 5:1-11.

Background Text: John 1:35-42.

Study Questions:

For Question 1, Read John 1:35-42.

1) How do we know Peter met Jesus before the event in Luke 5:1-11?

For Questions 2-8, Read Luke 5:1-11.

2) Luke records that Jesus sat down in Simon's boat to teach. Sitting down was a posture taken by masters, or teachers, as they taught. What makes Jesus' act of sitting important?

3) In John 1:41 we read how Peter's brother Andrew, told Peter he had found the Messiah, and then took him to meet Jesus. This tells us that Peter knew who Jesus was, and he knew that Jesus knew him. Time has passed and now Jesus is in Peter's boat (Verse 3). After He finishes teaching, Christ tells Peter to "Put out into the deep water and let down your nets for a catch." Peter answers "Master, we worked hard all night and caught nothing, but I will do as you say and let down the nets." When the word 'Master' is used as it is in this verse it always indicates a person

of high status. How does believing Christ is a person of high status instead of the Messiah makes it difficult for Peter to trust that Jesus knew where the fish were?

4) Some theologians believe Peter doubted Jesus. What do you think?

5) Philippians 4:6 reads, "Be anxious for nothing, but in everything by prayer and supplication, with thanksgiving let your requests be made known to God." Peter talks back to Jesus and questions if He

knows what He is talking about. There have been times in our lives that we have questioned what Christ has wanted us to do. How is taking our doubts to God in prayer, different from Peter's response to Christ?

The second part of Luke 5:5 reads "...but I will do as you say and let down the nets."

6) How does Peter's statement show obedience but not trust?

In verses six and seven we see the result of Peter's obedience to this teacher who is held in high regard. The outcome of this event changed Peter's life forever. Verse eight of Luke chapter five reads, "But when Simon Peter saw that, he fell down at Jesus' feet, saying, 'Go away from me Lord, for I am a sinful man!'" The Greek word used for Lord in this verse is *kyrie* from the Greek root *kurios*. Note: *kurios* is typically transliterated as *kyrios*. The definition of *kyrios* is "...supernatural master overall."[1]

7) How does knowing what *kyrios* means help us understand the shift in Peter's thought process from John 1:41 to his actions in this verse?

8) In verse eleven we read, "When they had brought their boats to land, they left everything and followed

---

[1] James A. Swanson, *Dictionary of Biblical Languages with Semantic Domains: Greek (New Testament)*, (electronic ed.), (Oak Harbor: Logos Research Systems, Inc., 1997).

Him." These fishermen walked away from a catch that would have provided them substantial income. What is the significance of walking away from this catch of fish?

Practical Application:

Think back to a time when trusting God made absolutely no sense. Record your thoughts about what happened. What was the circumstance? What did you do? What was the outcome? Record your response in the space below.

Summary:

As the cadet froze on the tower, Brent could see fear pouring out of every fiber of her body. He looked at her and with deep-rooted self-assurance said, "It's okay, watch me closely."

He explained that he was going to jump away from the tower and let go of the rope with both hands. He also told her to watch the speck at the end of his rope when he jumped. As he let go and jumped back, he yelled "falling." The speck wrapped itself in the rope, then ran in the opposite direction of the tower. When the cadet looked at Brent he was hanging in mid-air, hands-free, and smiling at her. Her body relaxed, and her eyes refocused. Brent locked eyes with her and they slowly walked down the tower together.

Each of us has questioned God, especially when asked to do something that makes absolutely no sense. That's what Peter did. He questioned Christ, but obeyed Him and then trusted Him. If you are stuck on a tower and afraid to move, don't be. Christ was there to help a fisherman from Galilee even as he doubted, and He is there for you. Trust Him, just like Peter did. Lock your eyes on Him and let Him walk with you the rest of the way down the tower.

LESSON 2

Boldness

Introduction:

What if I told you that Brent is a Christian, yet he doubts God? He trusts God to keep His promise about saving him through the blood of His Son, however, he doesn't allow Christ to be involved in every part of his life. He prefers to work through life's conflicts and adversity on his own. He is inflexible in his belief that God just doesn't understand life's events as well as he does. Here's an example:

Brent works as a part-time commissioned salesperson in an electronic retail store. God has blessed his hard work and he is constantly one of the top three salespersons (including those who are full-time). Brent passionately believes a Christian should strive to live a debt-free life which means he needs to graduate with no student debt. Lately, Brent has felt God calling him to help serve dinner at a homeless shelter. He knows if he commits to helping serve dinner at the shelter, he will be forced to give up at least one night of his retail work and will most likely have some educational debt to pay when he graduates. He is convinced that God doesn't understand what He is asking him to do, so when he prays, he makes sure to tell God how wrong He is. In short, Brent is bold enough to believe that he needs to correct God.

Would it surprise you if I told you Peter did the same thing?

Before we begin, let's read these passages to gain an understanding of this event.

Lesson Text: Matthew 16:13-23.

Background Texts: Mark 8:27-33; Luke 9:18-22.

Study Questions:

For Questions 1-3, Read Matthew 16:13-16.

1) Jesus is in the district of Caesarea Philippi and is alone with His disciples. He asks them a simple question "Who do *people* say that the Son of Man is?" Christ already knew who men thought He was, but by asking this question, He prepares the

disciples for a far more important question, "But who do *you* say that I am?" Up until this time our author (Matthew) has been quietly leading us toward the recognition that Jesus is the Messiah. He has shown us healing and miracles, but now he records this event to bring to the front who Jesus is. What made people think that Jesus was John the Baptist; Elijah; or one of the prophets?

2) When Christ asks His disciples "But who do you say that I am?" He is asking them to voice what He knows they are thinking. What is the importance of the disciples hearing each other declare that Jesus was not another prophet, but instead was the Messiah?

3) In verse sixteen, Peter, being bold and passionate declares "You are the Christ, the Son of the living God." It's easy for us as Christians to read what Peter said and think "Yup, you got that right. Jesus is the Son of the living God." But place yourself back into Jesus' time. Here is a man who is the son of a Jewish carpenter, with radical ideas about religion and how to practice it. If you heard Peter's declaration, what would you think?

For Question 4, Read Matthew 16:17-19.

4) Jesus responds to Peter in verses seventeen through nineteen. Pretend for a minute that you are Peter. How are you feeling after hearing Jesus' response?

For Question 5, Read Matthew 16:20-21.

5) In verse twenty-one, Matthew uses the words "From that time…" to indicate the passing of time. During this period Jesus began to show the disciples what the future held for Him. The word 'show' is the Greek word *deiknyein* which means to "...explain, show the meaning of something" [2] This verb is in the active voice which means the action does not stop but continues. Since the action continues, we know that from the time Peter made his declaration up to the moment of this event, Jesus continually told His disciples that He had to go to Jerusalem, suffer, and be killed. If you are a disciple and hear this from the man you know to be the Messiah, the one who has been sent by God to save Israel from its oppression, what would you be thinking?

---

[2] Swanson, *Dictionary of Biblical Languages*, Logos Research Systems, Inc.

For Questions 6-7, Read Matthew 16:22.

6) Peter began to rebuke Jesus. What would lead Peter to feel he had the right to rebuke the living God?

7) How do the words "God forbid it, Lord! This shall never happen to you." show Peter's boldness?

For Question 8, Read Matthew 16:23.

8) There are several theological positions concerning Christ's words "Get behind me Satan!" One position believes that Peter was being used by Satan and that Christ was rebuking Satan. Adam Clarke

and Albert Barnes, in their works on the book of Matthew, disagree with this view because the Greek word translated as Satan is typically used to designate an adversary. In short, Christ was telling Peter he was an adversary to His (Christ's) plans. How can Peter's words be seen as opposing Jesus' plan?

Practical Application:

Write about a time you have told Jesus you knew you were right and He wasn't. What was the result?

Summary:

Brent earnestly prayed about the homeless shelter every day for three months. His prayer focused on telling God how important it was to live debt-free, but if He (God) wanted Brent to serve at the shelter, He would need to make it vividly apparent to him. After three months of consistent praying, no vivid event occurred which led Brent to believe he needed to serve at the shelter. Brent felt a comfortable smugness in having told God He was wrong to call him to a ministry that infringed upon his work hours. At that precise moment, someone tapped on his dorm room door.

When Brent opened the door, his pastor was standing there. "I don't have a lot of time to visit, but this is important so please excuse me for being extremely direct." Pastor Mo's voice was fast-paced as he rushed on with his explanation. "The team that works at the homeless shelter needs someone to help serve dinner twice a week. The church typically does not ask college students to serve at the homeless shelter because of the time commitment, but we firmly believe God wants you to be involved."

After a short prayer, Pastor Ron hurried off to the next appointment on his overfilled day.

The quiet voice inside of Brent is now insisting that he acknowledge the visit from his pastor was no coincidence. Reluctantly, that night at work he asks to sit down with his sales manager. His heart begins to beat faster as he explains that God is calling him to serve dinner at the homeless shelter and he needs to have two specific nights off from work.

Brent's manager smiles at him and Brent feels sweat beading on his forehead. "Is there a small silent voice, quietly pushing you to have this meeting with me?"

As Brent's eyebrows involuntary arch toward the ceiling, he stammers "How…how…did you know?"

His manager explains that he often uses God's silent voice to manage the sales team. He also tells Brent the store owners are Christians and have a deep commitment to helping the underprivileged. Because of this, the store has a policy that allows a commissioned salesperson to be paid his average hourly wage while serving as a volunteer in the community.

As he walked away from the meeting, Brent's eyes stared at the ground while a pink flush began to creep up his neck. He realized his smugness was nothing more than his pride at work. God already knew where He needed Brent and what the store's policy was. This was a notable lesson for Brent and it can be one for us. The next time we want to tell God what He needs to do, let's remember this lesson. God is God and we are not.

LESSON 3

Self-Confidence

Introduction:

So far in this study, we have looked at the character traits of trust (or lack of it) and boldness. In this lesson, we are going to look at self-confidence.

Brent immensely enjoys the extracurricular activities offered by the R.O.T.C. program and has participated in a few of them. However, his deeply held passion for the close order drill team places it at the top of his favorites. This is Brent's senior year and he has been chosen as the commander of the team. The team is preparing for a regional drill meet which he is supremely confident they will win. He also knows that when they win, they will go to nationals for the first time in school history.

Each team has been given a series of commands that the commander needs to commit to memory and then execute during their two minutes on the drill field. Brent's team is small, but he knows he is on equal footing with all the other teams who will be attending, including those from a couple of the military academies. Brent's team has spent hours on the drill field practicing. He has memorized the list of commands until he can recite it backward. He knows deep in his soul that nothing could keep his team from going to nationals. However, his coach constantly cautioned him that he would be on an unfamiliar drill field and there was a chance he would become disoriented. Brent silently laughed at the coach's remark.

Just like Brent believes he knows himself better than his coach, Peter believed he knew himself better than Christ. This is the beginning of failure for both Brent and Peter.

Before we begin, let's read these passages to gain an understanding of this event.

Lesson Text: Mark 14:26-31.

Background Texts: Matthew 26:30-35; Luke 22:31-34; John 13:31-38; Zechariah 13:7.

Study Questions:

For Questions 1-3, Read Mark 14:26-27.

1) Jesus and the disciples have finished their last meal together in the upper room and are now at the Mount of Olives. Jesus turns to them and tells them "You will all fall away because it is written, 'I WILL STRIKE DOWN THE SHEPHERD, AND THE SHEEP SHALL BE SCATTERED.' " Anytime we see a quote capitalized in the New American Standard Bible, after the words it is written, it means the verse being cited is from the Old Testament. This particular verse is from Zechariah 13:7. Who is the shepherd in this verse?

2) Who are the sheep in this verse?

3) Imagine for a moment that you are one of the eleven disciples standing in the garden with Christ. You have spent the last three years at His side learning to serve and minister under His direct guidance. You have faced persecution and trials without turning away from His teachings. Now He quotes the prophet Zechariah and tells you that you are going to fulfill this prophecy. How do you feel?

For Questions 4-8, Read Mark 14:28.

4) After Jesus quotes Zechariah, He tells the disciples two important facts. What are they?

   a) He will be r_____.

   b) He will go ahead of them to G_____.

5) When Jesus tells His disciples these two things, He wants them to know four important facts.

   a) He will die, b) He will be buried, c) He will be raised from the dead, d) After He rises from the dead, He will meet them in Galilee.

   Jesus' statement seems to fly right over the heads of the disciples. What would cause them to not grasp what Christ was saying in this verse?

6) After Christ's death, the disciples go to Galilee – but they do not look for Christ. Instead, they go back fishing. What would cause them to forget what Christ told them to do?

7) How can this relate to you?

8) Although this is a small deviation from our main discussion about Peter and his self-confidence, we need to stop and ask ourselves an important question. What causes us to oftentimes have difficulty hearing what Christ says even though He is speaking plainly?

For Question 9, Read Mark 14:29-31.

9) Peter ignores what Christ has said about meeting them in Galilee and concentrates on the verse quoted from Zechariah. It is apparent that Peter is offended by Jesus saying he will be one of the persons who will fulfill the prophecy of Zechariah 13:7. If we paraphrased what

Peter said in verse twenty-nine, it might sound like this, "Hey even though those weaklings over there may fail to stand beside you, you can count on me." Jesus responds to Peter's outburst in verse thirty, telling him he will deny Him (Christ) three times before the cock (some translations use the word rooster) crows twice. Verse thirty-one tells us that Peter kept saying insistently (some translations use emphatically) that he would never deny Christ even if he had to die. The words 'kept saying' are from one Greek verb that is in the imperfect tense and the active voice. The imperfect tense tells us the action was never completed. This means that Peter emphatically said and kept on emphatically saying that he would never deny Christ even if he had to die. How could this be considered a statement that shows Peter has an abundance of self-confidence?

Practical Application:

At times, each of us has been self-confident in our Christian walk and has not heard Christ speaking to us. In the space below or on a separate piece of paper record one of those experiences and what you learned.

Summary:

Brent was convinced his coach was wrong. The team had put in the time, he had memorized the commands, and they were ready. Deep down in the depths of his being where he held his secret beliefs, Brent knew his team was going to win.

LESSON 4

Hopelessness/Self-Condemnation

Introduction:

The day had finally arrived! Brent led his team onto the drill field and received permission to begin. Three commands into the drill sequence Brent became disoriented and his mind went blank. As he moved the team aimlessly around the field, self-condemnation began to bury itself deep within his heart. After formally exiting the drill field, Brent found a private spot, sat down, and buried his head in his hands. As he began to relive each step of what had just occurred, his body began to shake with the force of his uncontrolled tears. He had failed his team, his school, and his coach.

Brent felt hopelessness and self-condemnation after his showing on the drill field. It's what Peter will feel at the end of this lesson. Although Peter ran away after cutting off Malchus' ear, he ends up at Caiaphas' house, gains admittance by way of John, then enters the courtyard and warms himself at a charcoal fire (John 18:18). It is here that he meets his ultimate failure and his life will change forever.

Before we begin, let's read these passages to gain an understanding of this event.

Lesson Text: John 18:15-27.

NOTE: This passage contains a point of tension. John records that Jesus is first lead to Annas who was the father-in-law of Caiaphas the high priest. Peter gains entrance to the courtyard where Annas is located. After Annas is finished questioning Jesus, he sends him to his son-in-law Caiaphas. John writes that Peter is still in the same courtyard when he fulfills Jesus' prophecy. How can Peter still be in the same courtyard if Jesus has been moved to Caiaphas?

There are a few theological positions that are held concerning this point of tension. It is possible that Annas and Caiaphas are in the courtyard at the same time but at different locations. This position holds that Christ was first taken to Annas in one part of the courtyard and when Annas was finished questioning him, was moved to another part of the court yard. It is unlikely this happened. In verse twenty-four we read "So Annas sent Him bound to Caiaphas the high priest." The Greek verb 'sent' (*apesteilen*) indicates that Jesus was sent out to Caiaphas. When Jesus was sent out to Caiaphas, he was taken to another location other than the one that Annas was at. Another thought is that this event happened at the special chamber in the temple courtyard set aside for the Sanhedrin and Annas' home shared the courtyard with the special chamber. It is unlikely this happened because a slave-girl was keeping the door (V17). The Sanhedrin would never allow a woman to guard the door to their official meeting site, let alone a slave girl. The position that is most commonly agreed upon is that the homes of Annas and Caiaphas shared a common courtyard. This position holds that Jesus was sent out from Annas' home, and traveled across the courtyard to Caiaphas' home.

Background Texts: Matthew 26:57-75; Mark 14:53-72; Luke 22:54-62.

Study Questions: It has been four weeks since the start of this study, let's take a small quiz (three questions) over the first three lessons.

1. List the three characters traits of Peter that we have studied up to this point. Hint, look in the introduction and if that does not help, look at the title of chapters one, two, and three.

    a. T_____

    b. B_____

    c. Self-C_____

For Questions 2-3, Let's Review Mark 14:27-31.

2. Jesus told Peter he would do something before the rooster crowed two times, what was it?

3. How did Peter respond to what Jesus said in Mark 14:30?

For Question 4, Read John 18:1-4.

4. In these verses, Jesus is in the Garden of Gethsemane. He prays in anguish over what he knows he must endure in the coming days, then wakes Peter, James, and John for the second time (Matthew 26:40-46, Mark 14:30-42, Luke 22:39-46). At the instant, Judas shows up with cohort (a cohort was the tenth part of a Roman Legion numbering between 400 to 600 men), and officers from the chief priests and Pharisees. Seeing this great multitude, Jesus went forward to meet them. Think of that for a moment, Jesus knows what he is going to endure (remember the prayer He just

completed) and instead of running away, moves forward to meet the crowd. What caused Jesus to move forward instead of running?

For Question 5, Read John 18:10-27.

Peter is true to his word and attempts to protect his Lord. He wraps his hand around the hilt of a sword and awkwardly attempts to defend Jesus. His inexperience sword handling causes him to cut off the ear of the Chief Priest's servant, Malchus. Jesus corrects Peter and as Luke tells us in his gospel (Luke 22:51), He heals Malchus's ear. After attempting to defend Jesus, Peter runs away with all the other disciples.

Peter and John end up at the high priest's house where John is known (John's father Zebedee was an Orthodox Jew who is mentioned in the Talmud [the Jewish set of civil and ceremonial law], was well regarded in the community, and a friend of Caiaphas the High Priest). [3] As John brings Peter into the courtyard, a servant girl asks Peter if he is not also a disciple of Christ. The servant girl's question causes lava to burn in Peter's stomach. He mumbles a denial and quickly moves to a charcoal fire in the courtyard. Having reached the fire safely, Peter attempts to force deep breaths down his tightly constricted throat as he realizes everyone here will stand against him if they find out he is a disciple of Jesus. Standing at the fire, he watches as an officer violently strikes Christ, and his eyes open wide with fear. The individuals around the fire look intently at him and finally one of them asks "You are not also one of His disciples, are you?" (V 25) Peter quickly and fervently denies having any connection with Christ. He feels the courtyard walls pressing in on him and squirms as he realizes he is going to get the same treatment as Christ if they find out who he is. Another servant who was in the mob at the garden immediately looks his way and quickly asks,

---

[3] Herbert Lockyer, *All The Apostles Of The Bible,* (Grand Rapids, Zondervan Publishing House, 1972), 72.

"Did I not see you in the garden with him?" (V 26) Peter's mind whirls; his heart is hammering and he begins to break out in a heavy sweat as he realizes he is a breath away from experiencing the hideousness treatment that Jesus is going through.

5. Peter is frightened about announcing he is a follower of Christ. Think about a time you were frightened about announcing you were a follower of Christ.

In Matthew 26:74 we see a detailed account of Peter's third denial. For Question 6, Read Matthew 26:74.

6. What did Peter's curse sound like? (If you think Peter cut loose with a bunch of swear words, please keep your response clean and use other words that

help us to understand what you are saying. Example: "I don't know that piece of human waste.")

For Question 7-8, Read Luke 22:60-62 and Matthew 26:74-75.

In Luke's gospel, we read that Jesus turned and looked at Peter after the rooster crowed. Jesus saw Peter (along with the other disciples) run away after He was arrested. Christ sees him in the courtyard and hears Peter denying Him with cursing and swearing. Just as Peter finishes, the rooster crows and Jesus looks directly at Peter. At that moment Peter realizes that Christ has seen and heard everything that Peter has done in the courtyard.

7. Following the denial, the rooster's crowing, and Jesus' look; Matthew and Luke record that Peter wept bitterly. In Greek the word "wept" is in the

indicative mood, aorist tense, with an active voice. This means it is a fact that Peter wept, it happened in the past (before Matthew or Luke wrote about it in their gospels) and he did not just shed a tear or two but continued to cry and weep with agony and mental suffering (the word bitterly means to weep with agony and mental suffering.)[4] What caused Peter to be in such agony over his failure?

8. Think about a time you failed someone you deeply loved. How did you feel?

---

[4] Swanson, *Dictionary of Biblical Languages,* (electronic ed.), Logos Research Systems, Inc.

Practical Application:

The gospel writers show us that the once bold and confident Peter is now filled with self-condemnation. In the space below write about a time when you were extremely confident you would never fail Christ, only to end up experiencing what Peter felt. Sometimes we allow thoughts of past failures to ghost through our memory. What is one of the thoughts that haunt you? Please use the space below to record your answer.

Summary:

Brent tried to tell himself he wasn't a failure, but each day that passed increased the burden of shame as he remembered his breakdown on the drill field. The weight of guilt and failure continued to pummel him until he made the soul-wrenching decision to leave the drill team. Peter is carrying the same type of guilt and shame. Luke records that after the resurrection, Jesus appeared to Peter (Luke 24:34). There is no written account of what was said. We only know that Christ met with him. However, afterward in Jesus' two recorded appearances to the disciples, the boastful, self-confident Peter is strangely quiet. We don't know what Peter was thinking, but we do know he hid behind his inner struggle. Eventually, Peter followed Jesus' command and went back to Galilee but he did not minister. Instead, the weight of his shame along with his inner turmoil drove him back to his comfort zone of fishing. His self-condemnation led him to believe he was a failure and that his ministry had ended. But, what did Christ have in store for Peter?

LESSON 5

Restoration

Introduction:

As Brent walked away from the R.O.T.C building after resigning, his body shook with the pressure of dammed-up emotions. Stopping on the edge of the sidewalk, he stared at a group of students without seeing them, focusing instead on the frozen wasteland lying deep in his heart. As he stood contemplating the bleakness, a small island of warmth appeared while he thought about the satisfying comfort of his life before he joined the drill team. Brent's eyes slowly refocused on the world as he realized there was a way to escape the darkness of regret and failure. He decided to move back to the comfort of his past.

As months went by, he realized that although the past provided comfort, it could not replace what had been burned away inside him that day on the drill field. Then one day Brent heard a faint whisper traveling through the stillness of the air. His heart began to push against his chest and he involuntarily began to move toward the tantalizing sound. He began to run, following the enticing lure, desperate to feed the deep longing at the core of his soul. Breathing hard, he slowed down and cautiously peeked around the corner of the R.O.T.C. building. What he saw shocked him to the very marrow of his bones.

In this lesson, we are going to see Peter has found a satisfying comfort in his past life. He is back in Galilee fishing along with some of the other disciples. Someone on the shore shouts instructions across the water to them. Peter along with the other disciples follow the directive, and as they begin to haul in the net, he climbs over the side of the boat then races to shore. What he found changed his life forever.

<u>Before we begin, let's read these passages to gain an understanding of this event.</u>

Lesson Text: John 21:1-17. NOTE: In verse one, some translations use the term Sea of Tiberias. The sea of Tiberias is another name for the Sea of Galilee.

Background Texts: Please read in this order: Matthew 28:1-10; Luke 5:4-6; 24:1-35; Mark 16:1-8.

Study Questions:

For Questions 1-2, Read John 21:1-6.

Christ appeared to His disciples twice and in Luke 24:34 we read that He also appeared to Simon (we don't know what the conversation was, we are only informed that he appeared to Simon). What we do not see during the two times Christ met with the disciples after His resurrection is the non-trusting, bold, self-confident Peter saying anything. He is completely silent. I believe Peter is still struggling with his actions in the courtyard. After Jesus' second meeting with the disciples, Peter and six other disciples go to Galilee and go fishing.

1. According to John 21:2, six other disciples are with Peter. In verse three Peter tells them he is going fishing and they say they will come with him. This means over half of the remaining disciples decided

to go fishing on the Sea of Galilee. What was the reason the disciples went fishing instead of engaging in ministry?

2. The seven disciples fish all night and catch nothing. They notice a person on the shore watching them but they don't recognize who it is. The person calls out to them asking if they have caught anything. They answer back with a disgruntled "No." The person tells them if they cast their net on the other side of the boat, they will find some fish. I think it is important to note Peter's response to the person on the shore. He didn't know who it was, but he does

what he is told to do. How is this different from his reaction in Luke 5:4-6?

For Questions 3-5, Read John 21:6-11.

3. Once the disciples throw out the net and begin to draw it in, they find it is full of fish and they cannot pull it to the boat. John immediately knows who the person is onshore and cries out "It is the Lord!" Peter hearing John, puts on his outer garment and makes a passionate charge for Jesus. It is obvious Peter had an overwhelming desire to meet with Christ. What caused Peter's headlong passionate charge for Jesus?

4. Verse nine reads "So when they got out on the land, they saw a charcoal fire already laid and fish placed on it, and bread." Peter sees the charcoal fire, and he sees Christ looking at him. He remembers the last time he stood at a charcoal fire and Jesus looked at him. What do you think is going through Peter's mind?

5. Christ tells the disciples to bring some of the fish they just caught. Peter went to the boat and "...drew the net to land." (V 11) Notice that Peter doesn't argue about fish already cooking on the fire, he just goes to the boat and draws the net to land. How do Peter's actions show a change from the inside out? *HINT: Think back to the first time Christ told him to throw his net on the other side of the boat.*

For Question 6-7, Read John 21:12-17.

6. After breakfast, Jesus turns to Peter and asks him three times if he (Peter) loves Him (Christ). A lot of theologians have expressed an abundance of theological thoughts about verses 15-17, and the fact that Jesus asked Peter if he loved him three times. As I've studied these verses I have often wondered if Peter was embarrassed because of his past actions. So, when Jesus asks him if he has a Godly (*agape*) love for Him, Peter mumbles back that he has a brotherly love (*phileo*) for Him. After all, how could Peter claim he had a Godly love for Christ when he did what he did at the High Priest's house? Jesus tells him to tend His lambs and then gently asks Peter a second time if he *agapes* Him. I imagine Peter feels the deep guilt and anguish feeding the fire in his burning cheeks as his tears threaten to overwhelm him. With his failure so clear and fresh in his mind, he mumbles once again "I *phileo* you." Christ tells Peter yet again to shepherd His sheep. Peter is no longer able to hold back his

anguish. His pent-up emotions over a lost opportunity, guilt and failure begin pouring from his eyes as his breath catches in his throat. It is at this point that Jesus meets Peter where he is at. I see Christ gently lifting Peter's head, gazing into his eyes with all the love, mercy, and compassion that only God can provide. Then meeting Peter where he is at in his inward journey, Christ gently asks a third time if Peter loves Him. However, this time He uses the same word for love that Peter uses, *phileo*. Peter is in great distress, but the love that he has for Jesus comes pouring out of his tormented soul in a passionate outburst. LORD YOU KNOW I *PHILEO* YOU! I can imagine Christ's eyes locked onto Peter's as he breaks into a bright smile, then tells Peter very slowly and clearly "Tend. My. Sheep." What do you think Peter is feeling as Jesus with those words restores him and tells him to go back to what He (Christ) has called him (Peter) to do? Please use the space on the next page to record your answer.

www.ingramcontent.com/pod-product-compliance
Lightning Source LLC
Chambersburg PA
CBHW070800050426
42452CB00012B/2432

CONTACT INFORMATION

Moments With Yahweh

1001 West Grassland Lane

Lincoln, NE 68522

Phone: 402-613-5826

Email: contacts@mwy4chuck.com Reference: Before the Rooster Crows with relief and begged Brent to take the team. Brent looked at his coach, then at the team. As he gave the command for everyone to move into position, he rubbed his eyes to clear them from the tears that blurred his vision. He had been restored.

We have just seen Christ do the same thing with Peter, and He does the same thing with us. When we believe we have failed, and run away, He meets us where we are at and restores us. John said it best in his first Epistle, chapter one, verses eight and nine, "If we say that we have no sin, we are deceiving ourselves and the truth is not in us. If we confess our sins, He is faithful and righteous to forgive us our sins and to cleanse us from all unrighteousness." We are restored by the power of Christ's blood! Let's never forget that!

The drill field seemed to swim before Brent's eyes as the blackness of his suppressed emotions threatened to overwhelm him. Gazing back into the caring eyes of his coach, the dam within Brent broke releasing all the hurt and self-imposed pain in an outward explosion. "THOSE GUYS TRUSTED ME! YOU TRUSTED ME! I FAILED!"

Coach kept his eyes locked with Brent's. He gently placed both hands on his shoulders and spoke quietly. "Do you remember what the prophet Isaiah told Israel in the forty-third chapter of his book? Verses eighteen and nineteen read, 'Do not call to mind the former things, Or ponder things of the past. Behold, I will do something new, Now it will spring forth; Will you not be aware of it? I will even make a roadway in the wilderness, Rivers in the desert.' We need to take Isaiah's advice. Let's not worry about the past, let's move forward into something new. I want you to walk onto that field and help those young men."

With his heart in his throat, Brent cautiously moved forward. The team saw him and stumbled over each other as they raced forward to greet him. The young man who had been attempting to call out the drill commands smiled face. There at the end of the field, eyeing him intensely was his old drill team coach. The old feelings of failure, guilt, and shame began to batter the carefully constructed wall he had built during the last few months. Without thinking, he began to involuntarily move forward. His slow hesitant steps turned into a jog, then into a frantic sprint until he came to a sudden halt beside his coach.

When the team stumbled through another set of jumbled commands, Coach casually remarked "Those guys are struggling out there. They need a strong commander who can take care of them on and off the field."

Brent felt his face burning and pushed down the passion that threatened to erupt from him, "Well it's not me. The last time I was trusted with leading a drill team, I failed."

Coach turned and with gentle intensity looked directly into Brent's eyes, "Yes you did fail, but that doesn't mean you'll fail again. You've learned a lesson since then and I know that standing beside me now, is a broken and humbled young man."

7. After this event, we never again see Peter working as a fisherman. What does Peter's restoration show us about our lost opportunities, failures, and Christ's acceptance of us?

Practical Application:

Are you in Peter's position? Have you failed or missed opportunities in some area(s) of your life? Do you believe you are no longer able to enter a church, let alone be used by God? How can you relate to Peter? Maybe you have never experienced what Peter experienced, but chances are, you know someone who is in Peter's position. Use the space below to record how you will move forward or help another person to move forward from their regret, lost opportunities, or perceived failure.

Summary:

As he peeked around the corner of the building Brent's jaw slowly dropped. The drill team had re-united, but it looked as if they were trying to walk through freshly laid concrete instead of the closely mowed grass of the drill field. Brent noticed the team's labored breathing and sweat-soaked clothes as they attempted to follow the muddled commands given. As he stood watching, a sixth sense made him quickly turn his head towards one end of the drill field. Time froze, and the blood drained from his